In The
SHADOW
Of The Cross

In The SHADOW Of The Cross

Trial By Doubt And Darkness

Egil Sjaastad

Translated from the Norwegian
by David Pugh

Marshall Pickering

Marshall Morgan and Scott
Marshall Pickering
3 Beggarwood Lane, Basingstoke, Hants RG23 7LP, UK

First published in the UK in 1987 by Marshall Morgan and Scott
Publications Ltd
Part of the Marshall Pickering Holdings Group
A subsidiary of the Zondervan Corporation

Originally published as 'Når troen prøves. Om anfektelse og
kamp i kristenlivet.'
Lunde Forlag, Oslo, 1979.

British Library Cataloguing in Publication Data

In the shadow of the cross
 1. Christian life
 248.4   BV4501.2

 ISBN 0–551–01446–6

Phototypeset in Baskerville 10/11 by Input Typesetting Ltd, London
SW19
Printed in Great Britain by Richard Clay Ltd, Bungay, Suffolk

4

Contents

Preface

In recent years my country, like others, has been exposed to a wave of Christian teaching emphasising armour, weapons, power, victory, worship, joy, harmony and so forth. I often wonder, however, whether this approach does not leave something important out of account. For what we frequently experience in practice is defeat, poverty, sorrow and sickness. And the worst of it is, perhaps, our discovery that we are still sinners. We still have the flesh, the old nature, to struggle with in weariness. It is thus hardly surprising that we encounter times of spiritual darkness.

This situation drove me to look through the Christian library of another, older generation in search of spiritual help both for myself and my students. It was then that I discovered that several of the old writers had journeyed deep into the word of God and had returned with a spiritual wisdom and experience that enabled them to counsel their own time – and ours.

This book is therefore a bucket drawn up from the well of the elder Lutheran tradition. I look into some of the ideas that three individuals have taught me to find in the Bible – Martin Luther (1483–1546), the Reformer; Christian Scriver (1629–1663), a German pastor; and Carl Olof Rosenius (1816–1866), a Swedish lay preacher and journalist. The common strand of their teachings is an emphasis on a correct balance between Law and Gospel. Faith has nothing to cling to but Christ's work and it is only on this foundation that we can have boldness before both God and man. All three also display a clear insight into the struggle that we call the Christian life.

Translator's Note

The central concept of this book is expressed by the Norwegian term *anfektelse* (German *Anfechtung*). As used by Sjaastad and others, there is no single English equivalent. Its main thrust is towards doubt of one's own salvation, the feeling of judgement and condemnation under the wrath of God. Another important element of its meaning is trial or testing, and spiritual darkness, attack, temptation and tribulation all qualify. We may therefore describe *anfektelse* as being the question to which faith is the answer. The assault on assurance of forgiveness is, however, always uppermost. My reply to this linguistic challenge has been to employ a whole quiverful of English words according to context.

Sjaastad quotes many hymns no doubt familiar to Norwegian churchgoers. These have sometimes been replaced by English equivalents in thought and feeling – mostly from the Methodist hymn book – sometimes rendered into prose, sometimes omitted. Scriver has been retranslated from the Norwegian translation used by Sjaastad; so too have most of the Luther quotations, as Sjaastad provides no references. Biblical quotations are from the New International Version.

David Pugh

Some Old Advice – For Our Time

'They say that they have been caught up to the third heaven – they tell of wondrous experiences.' Thus wrote Philip Melanchthon to Luther in his confinement at Wartburg. He was both excited and yet also somewhat uncertain and in need of his colleague's counsel. What had happened? Three men had arrived at Wittenburg with a singular gospel; they called themselves 'prophets', commissioned by divine revelation pure and simple. Charismatic experiences abounded, and it was now time, they said, for each and everyone to yield themselves to the unrestricted control of the Holy Spirit.

Luther answered his anxious friend with a sober appeal to Melanchthon's own judgement:

> 'I definitely do not want the "prophets" to be accepted if they state that they were called by mere revelation. . . .
> In order to explore their individual spirit, too, you should inquire whether they have experienced spiritual distress and the divine birth, death and hell. If you should hear that all [their experiences] are pleasant, quiet, devout (as they say), and spiritual, then don't approve of them, even if they should say that they were caught up to the third heaven.'

Here was something for the learned but confused Melanchthon to test the spirits by!

This Reformation cameo illustrates an important element in Lutheran doctrine. In the words of another Reformer, 'Evangelical Christianity is to be known by *the faith that is sorely tried*'. A religion that knows nothing of the trial by doubt and darkness is not, therefore, evangelical.

The term spiritual affliction or distress* is not often heard nowadays, but we meet it constantly in an older generation's edifying literature.

> 'Spiritual distress is the heaviest cross and the greatest burden that the just, holy, wise and good God sends His believers.'

These words are from Christian Scriver (1629–1663), who was familiar with the phenomenon and devoted a good proportion of his massive (2,000 page) *Treasure of the Soul* to it.

> 'When God decides to give His children wisdom and spiritual maturity, He enrols them not only in the school of the Cross, but in the university of spiritual distress.'

Through *Treasure of the Soul*, thousands of people, including many of my own countrymen, have found comfort and guidance for their Christian walk. Scriver is no polemical theologian like Luther, doing battle with superspiritual fanatics, but a counsellor who has aided anxious, doubting souls and has, thereby, contributed to the shaping of an evangelical Christianity.

Another writer, still well-known in Scandinavia, is the Swede, Carl Olof Rosenius (1816–1868). He puts it more bluntly still – 'the faith that is never severely tested, is false'. That his most widely read book is entitled *The*

Anfektelse. See translator's note.

12

Road to Peace is no coincidence, for the main burden of Rosenius' teaching was the guiding towards a full assurance of salvation of those who felt condemned by their conscience. He too knew what it was to have to fight his way through darkness and doubt. For Rosenius assurance and distress are nevertheless not simple opposites, for assurance is always a beleaguered but still fighting force. Full freedom from doubt and dread is not to be had this side of the grave.

One of the reasons why these older teachers spoke so much of cross and affliction was simply that they themselves had lived through many times of darkness. We recall Luther's great agonies of soul in the monastery. We remember how Scriver struggled with God because the superspirituals of his day called him an old hypocrite. Rosenius, too, was torn by conflict. From time to time he had to do battle with doubts of God's very existence, with melancholy and spiritual darkness.

Their own personal crises are not, however, the only reason for their speaking as they do. More important is their understanding of God's Word; the trial by doubt and fear was a pillar of their whole theology. Much modern teaching has waded into the spiritual shallows, away from the depths that the older writers sounded. In some circles the tendency is even to regard spiritual distress as something strange and unnatural. We may justly ask whether this approach does not betray an inadequate understanding and practical experience of Biblical truth.

The purpose of this book is to provide insight into what the Word says that spiritual affliction, the trial of faith, actually is. We will also examine what the older writers had to say about why a Christian should have to suffer it, and, more importantly, endeavour to locate the springs of comfort that God in His mercy has given His struggling children.

Anguish and Faith in the Bible

We often speak of 'heroes of the faith', and rightly so, for the Bible bears witness to a good many. These individuals were not, however, always spiritually joyful. On the contrary, they struggled and complained, were tried and afflicted. From some of their testimonies we may catch a glimpse of what the trial of faith actually is.

The Sons of Korah: 'As the deer pants for streams of water, so my soul pants for you, O God. My soul thirsts for God, for the living God. Where can I go and meet with God?'
(Psalm 42. 1–2)

David: 'How long, O Lord? Will you forget me for ever? How long will you hide your face from me? How long must I wrestle with my thoughts and every day have sorrow in my heart?'
(Psalm 13.1–2)

'O Lord, do not rebuke me in your anger or discipline me in your wrath. For your arrows have pierced me, your hand has come down upon me. Because of your wrath there is no health in

my body; my bones have no
soundness because of my sin.'
(Psalm 38.1–3)

Job:

'If only you would hide me in
the grave and conceal me till
your anger has passed! If only
you would set me a time and
then remember me!'
(Job 14.13)

Jeremiah:

'Why is my pain unending and
my wound grievous and
incurable? Will you be to me like
a deceptive brook, like a spring
that fails?'
(Jeremiah 15.18)

Paul:

'... but I see another law at
work in the members of my
body, waging war against the
law of my mind and making me
a prisoner of the law of sin at
work within my members. What
a wretched man I am! Who will
rescue me from this body of
death?'
(Romans 7.23–24)

'To keep me from becoming
conceited because of these
surpassingly great revelations,
there was given me a thorn in
my flesh, a messenger of Satan,
to torment me. ... But he said
to me, "My grace is sufficient
for you, for my power is made

perfect in weakness." Therefore I will boast all the more gladly about my weaknesses, so that Christ's power may rest on me.'
(2 Corinthians 12.7 and 9)

The trials that this little cross-section had to endure were of different kinds, but there are common factors nonetheless. They know that it is God with whom they are dealing, and so in their distress it is God to whom they turn. They complain, however, that He is hidden, that He has forgotten them and does not answer. Lord, how long? they cry; Why, Lord? They have encountered the wrath of God and discovered the abyss of depravity in their own hearts. The trial of faith has bowled them over, broken them in pieces and left them downhearted. Scriver has tried to distill the essence of these experiences:

'In spiritual darkness the soul is given to feel the wrath of God and the power of sin together with the fear of hell, darkness, dread, corruption, melancholy, despair and other gloomy thoughts.'

Many struggling believers will recognise their own state in these testimonies; either they have encountered the living God and have been dismayed, or else they are unable to find Him, He appears to be deaf or to have abandoned them. Those finding themselves in this terrible darkness may learn from the biblical heroes of faith, who cried out, but did not turn their backs on God. With Jacob they said, 'I will not let you go unless you bless me' (Genesis 32.26). The testing is not to be taken casually.

Typical of the men of great faith is that they cling to God's grace in spite of everything, right in the middle of the darkness. It is exhausting work, but still they cry

to God and do not let go their grip on Him even in the
Valley of the Shadow.

David: 'Out of the depths I cry to you,
O Lord; . . . But with you there
is forgiveness; therefore you are
feared.'
(Psalm 130.1 and 4)

Paul: 'What a wretched man I am!
Who will rescue me from this
body of death? Thanks be to
God – through Jesus Christ our
Lord!'
(Romans 7.24–25)

In the most impenetrable gloom they cling to God
and the riches of His grace. A Christian has to experience
a twofold life – that of joy and sorrow, affliction and
comfort, lamentation and thanksgiving. In Paul's words,

'sorrowful, yet always rejoicing; poor, yet making
many rich; having nothing, and yet possessing
everything.'
(2 Corinthians 6.10)

The men and women of the Bible knew praise, power,
joy and boldness and yet they also knew, from bitter
experience, that glory still lay ahead, 'We live by faith,
not by sight' (2 Corinthians 5.7) and ' . . . but we
ourselves, who have the firstfruits of the Spirit, groan
inwardly as we wait eagerly for our adoption as sons,
the redemption of our bodies' (Romans 8.23). Darkness,
testing and spiritual affliction belong to the pilgrimage
we are making; we still bear 'the old Adam' with us,
and have good reason to weep over our sins. Our souls
will know their dark night, bodily sickness will meet us

on the way, and physical death lies along our path. For the believer there is no escaping these trials.

Paul struggled and prayed several times to be free of something that especially troubled him, 'a messenger of Satan', as he called it. God's answer was strange and wonderful: 'My grace is all you need, for my power is strongest when you are weak' (2 Corinthians 12.9). These great men of faith knew distress – so that they might not lose the need for God's grace. God gives His children many hard lessons to learn, and not the least of these takes the form of a stripping-away of everything in the trial by darkness so that they have nothing left to cling to but 'the naked word' of God's mercy in Christ.

'Out of the depths I cry to Thee
Lord God O Hear my prayer!
Incline a gracious ear to me
And bid me not despair
If Thou remembrest each misdeed
If each should have its rightful place
Lord, who shall stand before Thee?'
Martin Luther

The Trial by Doubt and Darkness

The believer is frequently unable to analyse the trial he is undergoing. It is a matter of nameless unease, of fogs and mists, everything seems at once onerous and difficult to get to grips with.

We will nevertheless attempt to draw out some of the distinguishing features of spiritual affliction and the trial of faith as described in the Bible, in the Lutheran classics and in Christian experience.

The 'terrified conscience'

True Christianity is experiential – but not all experiences are valid proofs of a true Christianity. We have already encountered the superspirituality that emphasises unusual experiences. These are, however, by no means a guarantee.

The Lutheran Confession of 1530 – the Augsberg – goes to the heart of the matter, saying that the Gospel cannot be perceived aright without the struggle of the 'terrified conscience'. This is the struggle the German Reformers called *anfechtung*, spiritual distress, the trial of faith; they had encountered the Word of God in such a way that they were shaken by it; they understood that they were confronted with a holy God.

This crisis of the conscience is not an isolated phenomenon in the life of a Christian, but something which follows him as long as he lives. Not, however, in such a way as to make him morbidly obsessed with his own sinfulness, but letting him live in personal renewal or awakening – which is really nothing other than a quickening of the conscience. Through this inner revival we see so much of the depravity of our own hearts that the Gospel can never again be merely something responded to in the past but now outgrown. It becomes a permanent necessity.

Encountering the wrath of God

If revivalist Christianity is to be Biblical, it must not fail to proclaim the wrath and judgement of God over sin. That ours is a generation more or less unacquainted with the trial by darkness is, in the final analysis, probably due to failure to preach God's holy wrath with biblical earnestness. Consciences are no longer dealt such a rude awakening.

God is still a problematic issue and a stumbling-block to many, just as He was in Luther's time, but not on account of His jealous anger. Our contemporaries are more inclined to wonder whether He has anything in particular to offer man 'in this secular day and age'. The Word, however, turns the perspective upside down; the question *it* poses is whether God wants to have any kind of dealings with us at all. How may we escape His wrath at our sins, how may we find a God of mercy? (see Luke 18.13, Isaiah 6.5 and Ephesians 2.3).

> 'Might I in Thy sight appear
> As the publican distressed
> Stand, not daring to draw near
> Smite on my unworthy breast
> Groan the sinner's only plea
> God, be merciful to me!'

This is the voice of a man who has encountered God in His righteousness and His wrath.

God demands not outward works of the law, but a perfect heart, for His law is aimed at our hearts. For the sinner, to meet with the law is to meet with the wrath of God, he is 'weighed in the scales and found wanting' (Daniel 5.27). God calls man to account, and not one in a thousand has anything to say for himself (Job 9.2–3). We encounter what the older writers called the 'naked God', that is to say, we meet Him in His holiness when we are not 'clothed in Christ'. It is not, therefore, so strange that Luther describes the trial of faith in terms of 'assaults of dread of death and hell', for the heart of the matter is that it is, indeed, an encounter with God as Judge.

This is not an experience peculiar to the first steps of the Christian life, for we must constantly be unmasked as sinners and be made to understand how serious and hideous sin really is – serious enough to put our innocent Saviour under God's sentence. To walk in renewal is to be able to say:

'What have I then wherein to trust
I nothing have, I nothing am
Excluded is my every boast
My glory swallowed up in shame.'

When God and His holy law get too close to us, we become, in ourselves, wholly unrighteous, one hundred per cent sinful (c.f. Romans 7 on the effects of the law). The Reformers described the Christian as 'at one and the same time righteous and a sinner' – righteous in Christ, but sinners in ourselves. Retention of our cloak of righteousness in Christ requires us to be unmasked and to be seen for what we really are – sinners, fit only for the fire. The process can be exceedingly painful. In Luther's words,

'Sorrow and dread of God's wrath, fear of eternal death and of making the Devil's acquaintanceship in Hell, these permeate both mind and soul and weigh day and night upon the heart.'

Nor does Scriver pull any punches in describing this experience. At its worst, we may come to feel ourselves rejected by God, 'eternally, eternally, eternally lost'. When the sin in our hearts and the wickedness of our actions are revealed for what they really are, the wrath of God becomes a very present reality which we cannot escape except through Christ. For in Christ this wrath has been poured out in full measure and has achieved full satisfaction. 'Therefore, there is now no condemnation for those who are in Christ Jesus.' (Romans 8.1).

The Hidden God

Christians under pressure always find a mirror held up to their anguish in the penitential Psalms and laments of the Old Testament. 'Would you see a living portrait of the holy Christian church', said Luther, 'then pick up the Psalms.' One of their principal themes is a God who appears to have forgotten His believers, who seems to hide Himself. The psalmist feels cut off from God, he can see nothing but His wrath. 'You have set our iniquities before you, our secret sins in the light of your presence' (Psalm 90.8). His cry, 'How long will you hide your face from me?' ascends to God from the deep, but He does not hear. He is the 'hidden God', *deus absconditus*.

'I cannot find Him they call the soul's best friend', complains a Norwegian hymn. The sufferer seems to be spiritually dead, separated from God. It is, in Scriver's words, 'an experience of the pain and grief of the soul's eternal death'. Rosenius calls it God's peculiar 'concealment': God hides himself, withdraws His grace, gives us a bitter cup to drink, takes something dear away from

24

us, seems never to hear our prayers. These are the dark
winter days of the soul, as God lets us walk for a while
in spiritual darkness with neither light nor joy. Heaven
is shut in our faces, or so it feels, and in our despair we
cannot refrain from asking, 'Why, Lord?'

The worst of it all is that in His apparent withdrawal
we seem to be powerless against sin, and cross-grained
with both God and man. We feel reluctant to pray and
to read the Bible, and there is nothing left of us but a
sigh in the depths of our hearts – *Lord, deliver us*!

Lord, how strange

It frequently happens that we never receive any explanation of the whys and wherefores of this trial by darkness. God's thoughts are higher than our thoughts, His
ways are wiser. When He chooses to conceal the light
of His countenance, it is not for us to pronounce on His
reasons, for He is sovereign and unaccountable.

'Faith must be tested', wrote Rosenius, 'and that is
why the Lord leads His own on the strangest paths,
sometimes so strange that He appears to be taking
back again what He has expressly promised.'

It is during such periods that we see nothing but, as
it was once put, 'the bitter contradictions of our adoption
as sons of God'. That is, we read the Word and see for
ourselves what a high standing we really have as His
children, but what we actually *experience* is the very
opposite! It is as if God has gone back on His promises.
'They that are born of God', says Rosenius, 'are often
to be known by troubled hearts and weeping; they are
so full of sighs and lamentations that it seems as if they
are the most wretched slaves to sin and the devil'. That
God, who promises joy in the Holy Spirit, should lead
us on paths like these is difficult to comprehend. With

Paul we may call it *unsearchable* (Romans 11.33) – could it possibly be to teach us to rejoice, not in ourselves, but in God?

Since God is unaccountable, the Christian's lot in the world must necessarily be strange and mysterious – 'sorrowful, yet always rejoicing' (2 Corinthians 6.10). One of Rosenius' hymns captures this aspect of the Christian pilgrimage. 'What a paradox it is to be a believer', he says; 'to be so blessed yet to sigh so deeply; to be so exalted but see so little of it, to live in a fortress yet so seldom know peace.' We walk, as a rule, by faith and fail to see the Lord, we enjoy only for brief moments what we in reality possess all the time. Elsewhere he writes:

'To be a Christian means to be a child of God with whom He plays a very serious game – a little while, yet a little while, and you will not see me.'

In a sermon on John 16.16–23 Luther uses the same text, 'yet a little while' to support his teaching on the trial of faith. He speaks of 'losing Christ', and by way of comfort adds that according to Jesus' own words the trial is soon over. Christ draws away from us and lets our hearts remain in sin, death and the power of Hell, he says: God, the unfathomable, hides Himself. His grace is no longer apprehendable.

This 'game' that God 'plays' with His children is incomprehensible at the time, and not infrequently afterwards.

'It is a matter wholly opaque to reason', says Scriver, 'and to our sinful flesh, that God, who is called the Father of mercy and God of all comfort, can permit Satan so to shoot his arrows into the believer's heart.'

Those with any experience of these things must agree with Luther that 'there is a darkness over this abyss'.

Our task is, therefore, not to give way to despair in this 'thick, black gloom of faith' (Rosenius). Christ's kingdom is a realm of faith, and he who cannot do without seeing and touching may just as well take his hat and leave. As Rosenius puts it,

> 'Do not imagine that when undergoing the trial of faith you will be able to see any sign of your new birth – no one can see anything in the dark.'

When God conceals Himself, it is as well to have a higher and firmer footing than that which can be touched and seen.

Is your faith alive?

The Word says that a city built on a hill cannot be hidden, and that a branch that bears no fruit will be cut off and cast into the fire. One aspect of spiritual distress is just this, that we seem to lack all evidence of our being God's children. There is so little fruit of the Spirit in my life, we think, that soon God will decide to have nothing more to do with me.

This is not a matter to pass over lightly or to shrug aside, for the Bible is always concerned to point to the necessity of having a *living* faith. Merely cerebral knowledge has no power to save. As James says, 'faith by itself, if it is not accompanied by action, is dead' (James 2.17). We must be real-life Christians living the converted life with our God and must put our personal faith into action.

If, on the other hand, we begin to examine ourselves and compare ourselves with this standard, many of us will experience doubt and insecurity.

'Weary of earth and laden with my sin
I look at heaven and long to enter in
But there no evil thing may find a home'

Are we in fact living on 'cheap grace' in declining the struggles of conversion? For the gate is narrow and the way is hard, and it is therefore right to do as the old pietists taught and turn the searchlight upon ourselves.

The pietists' doctrine of the outward signs of a living faith may, however, turn into legalism. For when self-examination unmasks us as miserable and unworthy Christians, the remedy is not really a matter of simply 'pulling ourselves together', but of getting in touch with the Fountainhead; He alone can make our faith strong, living and fruitful. And the means for doing so is the Gospel itself. We must look to Him to whom the signs and tokens are supposed to bear witness.

Luther's remarks on the matter of outward evidence of faith were occasioned by his conflict with Roman orthodoxy. The Catholic tradition sees the doubt and anguish we have been discussing as an attack on our love of God. If the Christian's love of the Lord is the chief sign of his sonship, his assurance of salvation will easily come to rest on the answer to the self-scrutinising question, 'Do I *really* love God?' Luther, however, gets right away from this approach:

'For when Satan disputes with me whether God is gracious to me, I dare not quote the passage, "He who loves God will inherit the Kingdom of God", because Satan will at once object, "But you have not loved God!" Nor can I oppose this on the ground that I am a diligent reader [of the Scriptures] and a preacher. The shoe doesn't fit. I should say, rather, that Jesus Christ died for me and should cite the article [of the Creed] concerning forgiveness of sin. That will do it!'

For Luther the answer to this kind of trial by doubt is always faith in the 'principal article' of forgiveness of sins and adoption for Jesus' sake. It is this which makes the insecure Christian's faith a 'living, active thing', bearing fruit in good works.

The really serious question is, therefore, not 'Do I love God?' but 'Do I really trust in Jesus; is Jesus the chief need of my life? Do I display the principal characteristic of a living faith – *dependence* on Jesus?'

Physical trials

Personal afflictions, such as poverty, sickness, the anxieties of the world, disgrace, are all included in the concept of the testing of faith as used in Lutheran teaching. Luther called them physical, or bodily, trials. The Word of God tells of sickness that was not healed, of opposition from enemies, of tribulations and suffering of all kinds. These ills stem from the Fall and God's subsequent sentence on mankind (Genesis 3.17–19 et al.). All the world's sorrow is the consequence of God's 'mortification' of sin. On the individual level there is, of course, no necessary connection between tribulation and sin but, taking mankind as a whole, we can safely regard 'physical' trials as a result of the Fall and its curse.

Psalm Ninety exemplifies the correct perspective on suffering. The psalmist brings out the darker strands in the skein of human life, lamenting how quickly we fade away in trouble and vanity, how we live out our years to the bitter end 'with a moan', how we are snatched away as if by a flood, how like we are to the grass which flourishes but then is withered. And for the psalmist all this is God's doing. He even goes so far as to say, 'All our days pass away under your wrath'. All men – believers and nonbelievers alike – are in this situation because they belong to Adam's race, yet the heart-wisdom that enables us to understand this is the Lord's gift (v. 12). God must instil awe and reverence in us. We must fear Him as the Holy Lord and Judge because this is how He meets us in the harsh realities of this fleeting life, through our toil, through our bondage to the transitory, and through the iron grip of death.

In this way the physical trials transcend the physical; the light of the Word reveals them as an encounter with God's sentence on erring humanity. (This is not, however, all the Word has to tell us in our agony; there is comfort too, which will be discussed later.)

It is not easy to draw the dividing line between physical and spiritual affliction, for in both cases it is God with whom we have to deal. Physical tribulations are given depth by their spiritual significance, and purely spiritual trials can affect the body. Just as the hard-pressed psalmists found that their distress could drag them down into physical exhaustion, so we are also vulnerable to emotional and physical complications of the trial by doubt and darkness. The two kinds of testing will frequently be interwoven; we stand before God as naked beggars, with *all* the anguish of both body and spirit.

Death

These considerations show that the trial by darkness is, so to speak, a first cousin of death. Our anguished encounter with the wrath of God, said Luther, is an anticipation of judgement; 'death and hell live in His wrath'. We perceive God's just sentence on all sin, and realise that we ourselves ought properly to be damned.

At its deepest, spiritual distress is like the agony experienced in death. Conversely, death can be seen as the last and severest trial. For death is God's sentence on humanity after the Fall: 'when you eat of [the tree of knowledge of good and evil] you will surely die' (Genesis 2.17).

Death is not confined to the end of a life; on the contrary, its active power is felt long before in our human experience. Fully to confront the tragedy of death is to learn to recognise God's judgement on sin, for the agony of the conscience that knows itself under sentence is the best possible foretaste of death in all its frightfulness. Our consolation in facing death is thus the same as that which we have against what Luther called, the 'higher spiritual distress'. The sting of death being sin (1 Cor. 15.58), our comfort in both death and condemnation is the gospel of the forgiveness of sins in the blood of the Lamb.

> 'The fear of death, the despair, the dread – this is the real death'

> 'When Moses works in us, that is, when the Word of God unmasks sin and reveals His wrath, Moses is a servant of sin, death and wrath. For then it becomes clear that the divine wrath has brought us death. Hens and geese know neither condemnation nor fear of death as the final enemy, for they have no sin.'

These Lutherisms delve deep. This death-perspective on the trial of faith is not, however, experienced by all; it is, he writes, only a few that feel death impending and the divine wrath hanging over them. A deep recognition of the holiness of God and the seriousness of sin will nonetheless give Christians an inkling of this valley of the shadow. They must then strive to secure the right consolation.

Cross and tribulation

To be a follower of Christ is to live in tribulation and in the shadow of the cross. 'You form us through cross and tribulation for Your kingdom', we say in the

Norwegian liturgy. The cross and the trial of faith are related; the cross is our first and foremost encounter with the treatment the world metes out to Christians. It may also demonstrate the incomprehensible burdens God lays upon us. Jesus spoke in great earnestness of His disciples taking up their crosses and following Him. 'Christian' and 'cross' should be said in the same breath. Scriver describes three ways of carrying the cross.

'The cross humbles. Many take it up with reluctance, sighs and tears. They say, I *must* suffer, there is nothing to be done about it. Others take up their cross and bear it with patience, but still regard it as a burden they would gladly be rid of. They say, I *can* suffer, God gives me strength. Yet others not only take up the cross willingly, but love it and know that it is a mark of discipleship. They say, I *will* suffer, I love the cross, it comes from my Father and my Saviour has carried it before me.'

Christianity is 'the theology of the Cross' which, among other things, means that the trial by doubt and darkness is an integral part of our life in this world.

Some have a large cross to bear, others a small. Some have to bear their cross for a long time, others only briefly. Some have a hidden cross, others one that everyone sees. Following Jesus means that we cannot escape His cross – we cannot deny His atoning death for our sins. The main thing is to follow Him – whatever it costs.

Why, Lord?

Lord, how long? Why, Lord? David clenches his fists. Shall I be cast away forever from the clear light of your mercy? Tears blink in his eyes. If only God would show me the reason for this darkness! If only He had a word, a divine word, that could comfort me with the knowledge of its purpose. The player hangs his harp on the wall, weeping. He who lulled Saul with his playing, wails in his turn for a bard with solace in his strings. He craves answers for his burning question – why?

Speculation and theory as to the whys and wherefores of the trial by doubt and darkness can easily lead us astray, but the Word of God does, nevertheless, have something to say to us. It has some light to shed.

The role of Satan

Scripture treats Satan and his infernal hosts as a reality, and so must the Christian. We know that Satan is out to get us into his power, that this is his primary goal. When he tempts, the aim is to make the believer stumble, or better still, to fall from grace. Whenever someone loses that vital contact with God, the enemy of God has won a victory. Does Satan, therefore, play any part in spiritual trials and darknesses?

The Catholic tradition assigns the devil a considerable role. If the enemy achieves his goal the trials destroy the victim's Christian life. If however, he stands firm in temptation, without turning his back on God, the attack

is counted as something God has turned to the good –
tentatio probationis, the testing of the believer.

The Lutheran church has a more satisfactory explanation, in which Satan's role is subordinated to God and His wrath. Luther, for example, writes that

> 'In all trials and sufferings man should first of all run to God and confess that they are sent from God and receive them as such from Him – even though they come via the devil or other people.'

The psalmists, he says, accept the enmity of men as being not from them, but from God. This is, in fact, typical of several of the lamentation psalms; God can withdraw, as it were, leaving the man alone with his enemies. In the same way we can be left alone with the devil. Among other examples Luther uses the Temptation in the Wilderness to show how God can wholly abandon a person into the hands of Satan. Similarly with Job:

> 'The Lord said to Satan, "Very well, then, everything he has is in your hands. . . . Very well, then, he is in your hands. . . ." ' (Job 1.12;2.6)

Satan can, therefore, play a major part in spiritual distress, which may accordingly seem like a downright battle with the devil. Luther compares this struggle with that fought by Christ on His descent into Hell. Now, it is obvious that Satan's purpose is an evil one. He aims to make us founder in sorrow and despair. In the language of the Psalms, he torments the heart with fiery, poisoned arrows. Should he succeed in drawing us away from faith in Jesus, the trial does indeed become one of his accomplishments, and a tragedy. He is, after all, the enemy of God.

Even so, the omnipotent God knows how to make use

of Satan and his assaults, redirecting the evil to serve His own good purposes. Scriver can therefore echo Luther and say,

> 'It is Satan who is active in spiritual distress. But God is behind him.'
> 'God has given you into Satan's power.'

God permitted Paul to be harassed by an angel of Satan (2 Cor. 12.7). The enemy of the soul must therefore be unable to harm a child of God – provided only that he holds fast to God and His grace. In the end Satan reaps only shame and defeat, his fiery darts consume, according to Scriver, nothing but our pride and the lusts of the flesh. He is, of course, fearsome, but God's power is the greater, as the believer will find if he clings to God throughout his anguish.

Satan frequently uses God's own law to attack the believer, wielding it in accusation against the Christian's life and walk. The idea is to make us lose heart; the indictments are often correct, finding our sore points. But God can also turn these accusations to the good, for He has given us a mighty weapon, 'the eternal truth about Jesus – one died for all, You died for all, You died for me' (Rosenius). Therefore, when Satan tries to draw us into bondage under the Law he is to be met with the gospel of Jesus.

For God, the purpose of the Law is to show how vital it is for us to receive His righteousness to cover us. Through the Law we become, not pious but merely guilty (Romans 3.19ff). All this, however, serves God's overriding purpose of driving us to Christ. Satan's aim, on the other hand, is to drive the believer to despair, to stop him finding comfort in Christ – to hear him tell himself that he may just as well give in.

Our flesh, the 'old self', is in alliance with the devil, giving him a further, indirect, part in the struggle between flesh and Spirit. 'For the sinful nature does what is contrary to the Spirit, and the Spirit what is contrary to the sinful nature' (Galatians 5.17). Satan fights on the side of the flesh, so we must arm ourselves with strong weapons for the struggle.

Christ underwent the battle with Satan in the days of His flesh, and if Satan could assault the Son, he will do the same to His disciples. We cannot expect easier terms. In Rosenius' words, 'As He was, so are we also in this world'.

Attack as God's instrument

Even though Satan does play a part in these assaults and trials, it is God who is ultimately responsible. He does not intend to let the believer slip away from the experience – that is reserved for the last trial, death. A life without the testing of faith is, according to the Lutheran masters, an extremely dangerous thing. The devil is at his most active when we are *not* being tried and are inclined to feel secure in ourselves.

Trial by doubt and darkness is to be understood strictly theocentrically, as a tool in God's hands. At bottom it is His will that evil, His enemy, has a finger in the pie. God then turns it to the good. Trials and assaults have for this reason been called 'the heavenly Gardener's pruning knife'. The victim is in the divine workshop. Unless they break with God, even Satan's malice can serve God's children. Admittedly this is not easy to understand; these are God's thoughts, which are higher than our own.

God renders us helpless

Christian Scriver has attempted, in a semi-poetic style, to describe the way God deals with His children:

'Whom He would make to fear God, He makes a despairing sinner;
Whom He would make wise, becomes a fool;
Whom He would make strong, becomes a weakling;
Whom He would make alive, He thrusts into the maw of death;
Whom He would bring to heaven, He sinks into the pit of Hell.
Who would be great, becomes small.
He does not always bear His own in a palanquin,
For then they would slumber and forget to believe, pray and hope.'

These rather extreme formulations shed light on the purpose of the trial of faith. God wants to teach us to renounce all our human pride and strength before Him, we are to be made as little children who do not murmur against God and His Word. However pious and attractive they may seem, all the accomplishments of the 'old Adam' are hostile to God. It is God's will that we learn emphatically to renounce all attempts at self-sufficiency. This lesson is not learnt overnight, but God knows better than any of us that it must be repeated over and over again as long as we struggle with our sinful nature – in other words throughout our lives.

We are to be left with nothing to hope for but God and His mercy; helpless and therefore receptive to His aid. If He does not help then all is lost – 'who may then be saved?'. We must learn to say:

'Nothing in my hand I bring,
Simply to Thy Cross I cling.
Naked, come to Thee for dress
Helpless, look to Thee for grace . . .
. . . Rock of Ages, cleft for me
Let me hide myself in Thee.'

Self-confidence has been dealt with, God has made us helpless. We can say with Hanna, the mother of Samuel,

> 'The Lord brings death and makes alive,
> He brings down to the grave and raises up.'
>
> (1 Samuel 2.6)

Conviction of sin

As we have seen, the Law drives us into the darkness of the encounter with God as Judge. The believer is not, indeed, under the Law, but the Law acts nevertheless to keep him in a living awareness of sin.

> 'Now we know that whatever the law says, it says to those who are under the law, so that every mouth may be silenced and the whole world held accountable to God. Therefore no-one will be declared righteous in his sight by observing the law; rather, through the law we become conscious of sin.' (Romans 3.19–20)

God's purpose is to show us something of this truth in practice.

> 'My good works they are worthless quite,
> A mock was all my merit
> My will hated God's judging light
> To all good dead and buried
> E'en to despair me anguish bore
> That nought but death lay me before
> To hell I fast was sinking.'
>
> Luther

No-one can have a living Christian faith without humiliation and a constant need for God's grace. Mere head knowledge of our corrupt nature helps but little in the long run, for it is only through experience that we really come to see the truth about ourselves. When a Christian soul becomes utterly wretched, darkened and confused, says Rosenius, it is only then that it finally learns what *man really is*. And further,

> 'If you cannot be kept humble, but begin to think rather well of yourself, God will let a devil loose on you, let you meet with fierce temptations, yes, even let you fall into sin and disgrace. But the loss would have been greater had you been left to your pride, for with pride all is lost.'

Conviction is, therefore, one of the reasons for the trial. It is not, however, an end in itself. The point of it is, of course, to drive us in our anguish to Christ. For only Christ can help us meet God's wrath and judgement; He took both wrath and judgement in our place. Deep conviction leads a person into that total helplessness where he must stake everything on the *Atoner alone*. Through faith in Him we are stripped of all that is our own, and through faith we can stand confidently before God.

> 'That blessed sense of guilt impart
> And then remove the load;
> Trouble, and wash the troubled heart
> In the atoning blood.'

Conviction of sin must be on our prayer-lists. For the 'poverty of the Spirit' must be constantly nurtured if Christ is to become and remain our only solace. It is so easy to come to God towing a load of good works or religious experiences behind us as a kind of guarantee of our status, but it is very dangerous. He sends us trials and tribulations so that all false foundations may be torn down and that we may learn to build only upon the mercy in the heart of God. The pangs of conviction may then become songs of thanksgiving.

Building on the Word alone

In the trial of faith God often appears to be acting contrary to His word. We experience the direct opposite of what the Word says we are; it tells us that we are God's children and walk in fellowship with Jesus, but we feel nothing of the sort.

Christ Himself lived the same contradiction; He was the Son of God, but did not even have a stone to lay His head on. He was innocent but condemned as a malefactor. And His followers will meet a not dissimilar fate. The older Lutheran writers were even so bold as to claim that God apparently acts contrary to His express Word and promises.

It is of great importance at times like these to learn to hold fast to the Word alone, for the Word gives us the correct picture of our status as Christians. Feelings and experiences fluctuate, by no means always reflecting our true situation and exalted position as children of God.

Many say to themselves: I have both heard and read what the Word has to say on this, and I have prayed and besought God for clarity and for better weather in my Christian walk. In my weakness I have truly sought Him with all my heart, but it doesn't seem to help, my heart is just as it always has been – cold, dry, dead and full of sin.

There is only one remedy for these pains – the Word. God leads us on these apparently incomprehensible paths so that we may learn to cling to His Word *despite everything*. We must learn to pay more attention to God through His Word than to our own feelings and experiences. At bottom, therefore, trials, tribulations, assaults, doubts and darknesses are part of God's training in faith; trust in the Word alone must be strengthened in us.

The story of Abraham and Isaac serves as a powerful testimony to God's purposes in our spiritual affliction. Abraham learnt, through testing, to rely on God's naked promise, despite the command to sacrifice the son of that promise. He learnt reverence and obedience – 'now I know that you fear God' (Genesis 22.12). And Abraham's fear of God was expressed in submission to, and dependence on, God's Word alone.

Many Christians lack a true assurance of their salvation, their faith is sorely tried. God means to teach us to found our assurance on the Word, so that we may learn to build on the one and only and perfect foundation – its testimony to Jesus. By faith in Him we are 'blessed even though we sigh and sorrow'. Doubt and condemnation drive us to the foundation and bulwark of assurance, the Gospel of the death and Atonement of Jesus Christ.

It is often quite impossible for a Christian to see any improvement in his walk with the Lord. He seems to lack all the outward signs of regeneration and sanctification. In his heart he finds no charity towards others, or at least not towards the more unlovable, and his love of God is conspicuous mainly by its absence. He sees nothing but his evil, corrupt human nature.

'I have long withstood His grace
Long provoked Him to His face
Would not hearken to His calls
Grieved Him by a thousand falls'

Moments like these give birth to wonder and gratitude:

'O how shall I the goodness tell
Father, which Thou to me hast shared?

41

> That I, a child of wrath and hell
> I should be called a child of God'

The remedy is in the Word alone, not in feelings:

> 'I take God at His word and deed
> Christ died to save me, this I read.'

Pruning the branches

The Bible has much to say about God's chastisement:

> 'The Lord disciplines those whom he loves
> and he punishes everyone he accepts as a son.'
> (Hebrews 12.6)

And in every age it has been a favourite theme of counsellors and teachers.

> 'The believing soul is cleansed and smelted in the flame of trial and darkness so that there is nothing left but a great sigh – I am nothing, Lord! You are everything.' (Scriver)

Both the Bible and the devotional writers use image and simile to describe this aspect of spiritual distress; the gold refined in the fire, the tree that the heavenly Gardener prunes, the clay in the potter's wheel, the son under his father's rod.

> 'Hypocrisy', says Scriver, 'is so deeply rooted in the heart that it cannot be consumed except by the fire of spiritual distress. Through trials the flesh is weakened and subdued, but the spirit fortified and exalted.'

The trial of faith thus yields the fruit of Christian growth;

indeed growth is rarely a result of anything else. Roses grow only among thorns.

'When God decides to give His children wisdom and spiritual experience, He enrols them not only in the school of the Cross, but in the university of spiritual distress.'

In God's workshop the believer is made into a vessel of God's glory. Scriver uses another contemporary illustration; when a maid scours a tabletop, she scatters sand and ashes on it, adds lye and scrubs both vigorously and thoroughly. God in His goodness does the same to the believer's heart so as to scour it clean.

The 'Christian personality' cannot be formed without trials, testings and assaults, for these are all a part of the process of sanctification. Periods of sorrow, suffering and spiritual darkness are really intended to cleanse and scrub us, to put the flesh to death. This daily mortification of our old self gives the Spirit of God room for His sanctifying operations. Let us never pretend that this process is not a painful one; the battle of flesh and spirit is anything but a game. Its purpose is, however, good. 'Spiritual distress puts pride to death', says Luther, 'and nurtures a humble spirit in the believer.' Humility comes only through humiliation.

The process of cleansing and chastising has no end this side of the grave. God's training lasts a lifetime. He does not finish the treatment until it is interrupted by death. No-one can claim to be the finished product. The Christian life is one of constant *becoming*: as long as we are on earth we are in the process of becoming what God wants us to be. Not before Resurrection Day do we finish becoming.

The imitation of Christ

Jesus' temptation in the wilderness and His death on the Cross have, in all ages, been vital texts for any discussion of the trial of faith; for a Christian may not expect better treatment than Christ's. In an exegesis of Psalm 38 Luther says that:

> 'For the fiery arrows and the wrath of God make the heart's sin present and visible, whence comes inner unease and fear in all faculties of the soul. And the hand of God, or the outward effect of His punishment, makes the body utterly sick and wretched. When this is the case, everything is as it should be, for this is what Christ experienced.'

These are hard words, but even if somewhat exaggerated, they still contain a profound truth. To be conformed to Christ is to participate in His suffering.

On the cross Christ was reprobated and afflicted by God Himself, and He cried, 'My God, My God, why have you forsaken me?' He suffered wrath and knew anguish. A Christian will also enter into periods of Calvary darkness. 'Yes, if we are to rise with Christ', said Luther, 'we must die under God.' Our baptism into Christ's death and resurrection (Romans 6) involves, among other things, a life in death and resurrection – a life in which we are likened to Christ and experience the dark of judgement over our old self. And then the morning sun of redemption will give us resurrection, life and power.

'You must be likened unto Christ', says Luther, 'either here on earth or else in Hell.' We must, he asserts, be darkened and condemned under the cross before we learn to believe in and look up to the darkened and condemned Christ. Discipleship belongs with faith; the trial by darkness is an experience of discipleship that keeps us firm in 'faith alone', faith in 'Jesus alone'. Should we not come to faith in this life, however, death will lead us into the eternal condemnation under God's judgement. There we will be likened to Christ in His condemnation, but not in His resurrection – a terrible condition.

When Jesus says 'Follow me!' we are called into a rich and good life, but also into the struggles and trials of discipleship. Being likened or conformed to Christ is a painful process in which we share Christ's portion – in suffering, degradation and humiliation. 'Come to Jesus and be happy!', is a common approach. From one point of view it is a correct one, for we enter into a happy state, the state the Bible calls 'blessed'. But note *who* it is that are called 'blessed': the poor, the sorrowing, the meek, the hungry and thirsty, the persecuted (Matthew 5.1–11). Why is this? Because these share in Christ's humiliation. This ought to come as a shock for those who cannot recognise themselves in the Beatitudes.

To God's glory, Satan's loss and man's benefit

Those undergoing the trial by doubt and darkness have difficulty understanding how they can witness to God in that condition; they can neither love, hope, pray nor act as they ought. But in the heart of a true Christian a love of God and a faith in Jesus will nevertheless live on, even if half-buried. This, says Scriver, honours God and glorifies His name. The sufferer may not be able to see them himself, but the faith and the love are visible to God.

The sinner in the house of Simon the Pharisee had, no doubt, experienced the darkness of conviction under the wrath of God. When she was allowed to cling to Jesus and the words of His gospel, her love grew. And then she gave the glory to God, not to herself. The terrified consciousness of sin serves to strip men of their own honour, so that they may honour God and Him alone. In this way we may speak of spiritual distress as enrolled in the service of God's glory.

'God's goodness is never more glorious than when we have properly tasted God's wrath.' (Scriver)

As God is honoured, the devil is hindered. Satan can get nowhere with the childlike faithful who hold on to God in the middle of their distress; they cry, lament, pray and cling – to Him. And God is Satan's vanquisher. Let the devil appear as an angel of light (2 Cor. 11.14), or as a roaring lion (1 Peter 5.8), still he is unable to tear the lamb from the hands of the Chief Shepherd. As long as the believer fights in God's armour and with God's power, the devil can only suffer defeat.

The messenger of Satan that assaulted Paul drove him to even greater heartfelt prayer and to the gospel of God's grace. Through this experience Paul grew strong – strong in the Lord. All Satan's work was turned to good. Whoever is driven to Christ by Satan's attacks and accusations triumphs over the devil. This is the Saviour's greatness.

Scriver makes a rather strange comment, but, I think, a valid one, on the significance of spiritual distress for other people: 'The trials show them that Christianity is not just words, but power.' The victim seems impotent and wretched, but if he nevertheless keeps faith through his spiritual night Christianity is shown to be more than mere theory. God's power is made perfect in weakness. This power reveals itself as working endurance, patience, a sound mind and steadfastness in prayer. Let this serve to inspire us all to faith and prayer.

The self-satisfied, who think faith the easiest thing in the world, may find food for thought in an encounter with someone undergoing the testing. May there not be something missing in their self-knowledge? The Word of

God says clearly that it is right and proper to have assurance of salvation, but this is not at all the same thing as self-confidence. By their testimony the victors in the trial of faith can demonstrate that self-satisfaction must be distinguished from assurance. True assurance is security in Jesus. We need, perhaps, the exhortation, 'Examine yourselves to see whether you are in the faith; test yourselves' (2 Cor. 13.5). Those who keep the faith through the trial of doubt and darkness can be a living exhortation to us.

Solace in the Darkness

Many great hymns have been brought to birth in that moment when the light of the Word reaches into the darkened mind. The paralysing fogs of trial and doubt must yield to the rising Sun of the gospel. A divine wonder indeed!

The Gospel

The previous chapter touched indirectly upon the comfort we may find and cling to in our testings, whose purpose is, in fact, none other than to drive us to the true comfort and hold us there. Trials and tribulations have no other end in view than this, they serve only to drive us to the gospel; or to put it another way, to provoke the hunger and thirst that make the gospel into real spiritual food.

It is, therefore, *the Gospel* with which we must comfort ourselves and others. No feeble thing this, but the power of God. To those who are perishing the Gospel is, indeed, a foolishness and they find no use for it (1 Cor. 1), but for the believer it is able to draw the sting from trials and assaults. It has the power to take him from death to life and to shine into the most profound darkness of the spirit. How, then, does the gospel meet the sufferer? With the words, 'if God is for you, who can be against you?' (Romans 8.31). You think everything is uphill and contrary, and the worst of it all is that your own heart testifies against you. But listen, who can really be against you when you cling to God? He is *for* you!

The gospel also tells us that it is God who acquits. 'Who will bring any charge against you, whom God has chosen?' (Romans 8.33). If the whole world judges you guilty, if Satan accuses you, if men testify against you, if your heart says that you are too far gone for God's grace in Christ to apply to *you* – know then that God is the acquitter. And He acquits all those who in their anguish take refuge in Jesus. You are, indeed, a miserable sinner, but hold fast to Jesus, believe on Him who declares the *ungodly* righteous (Romans 4.5): from that moment on you are not accounted guilty of anything, you are 'blessed' even in the middle of your darkness. For your sins have been forgiven. In front of the hosts of heaven God Himself passes judgement and says – 'this one goes free'. Think of it, you are acquitted by the High Court of the universe!

The Gospel also says that Christ died for you, that He was condemned in your place. He was accursed instead of you. He was made sin for you (Galatians 3.13, 2 Corinthians 5.21). And then He rose again and sits at the right hand of God to make intercession for you. He rose and is defending you (Romans 8.34) – who can then condemn you? Not Satan, for he is trodden down by the defence Himself (Colossians 2.15). Not other men, for their verdict cannot convict where Christ is defending. Not your own heart, for that is not the supreme court. No, hear this, says the Gospel, you who are distressed and in fear: you are guilty and liable to death and damnation, but the sentence has fallen on *another*; cling only to Him, and you will never in all eternity face condemnation! You pass through judgement without being convicted. This is the Gospel of Christ.

'Hope therefore in my God will I
On my deserts not founding
Upon Him shall my heart rely
All on His goodness grounding

What His true Word doth promise me
My comfort shall and refuge be
That will I always wait for.'

Luther

It is, therefore, the biblical doctrine of justification that is most profoundly able to free the captives, and to grant us aid against the 'higher spiritual distress' when we doubt our salvation. Into the anguish of conviction comes the gospel of the 'attribution of righteousness' – Christ's own righteousness that covers the sinner from head to foot. Through faith in Jesus he becomes one hundred per cent righteous in God's sight, the utterly imperfect is simultaneously wholly perfect. 'There is but one way to escape condemnation', says Luther, 'to believe and proclaim with confidence, "Thou Christ art my sin and my condemnation".'

Christ is your *substitute*; what you did not do and could not do, He did in your place. What you could do and did do, He took the consequences of. No richer solace for the distressed is imaginable. The expression 'the blessed exchange' was once heard regularly from the pulpit, signifying that Christ and the sinner have changed places. Everything that is impure, sinful and unworthy about you has been accounted for and punished in Christ. Everything He is and has, His perfect life, His righteousness, His obedience and atonement for the world's sin, all this He gives to us. He clad Himself in our filthy rags, we shall be clothed in His shining white robes; in truth a blessed exchange.

When we grasp Christ in faith, at once we realise God's wrath against sin and triumph over it through forgiveness. With God's Word, the Gospel, says Luther, we struggle with God Himself and 'rescind His wrath'. Whoever has learnt this, he adds, is a doctor of theology.

Few have taught solace in 'Christ for us' – the Gospel of Christ's work for us – as well as Rosenius. In simple but powerful words he carries us from 'grace in my heart' to the safer 'grace in God's heart'. We must learn above all to build our Christian life on firmer foundations than our own spiritual accomplishments. In the face of everything we see and feel, we must find the true solace of salvation *in Christ*.

'It is particularly in such experiences of spiritual distress that it is necessary to have a higher and firmer foundation for faith than what we can see and feel inside us – a foundation wholly outside and above ourselves – namely that we constantly and unceasingly fix our eyes, through the Word, on what God Himself has said and done concerning our adoption as His children.'

'Christ in us' – that is, all signs of fellowship with Christlike feelings, experiences, fruits and so on – can never be sufficient to comfort us. Through the trial by darkness we learn to disregard these testimonies and hold fast to grace. Sun and cloud often succeed each other in the heart, says one of Rosenius' hymns, today I am renewed, tomorrow cold and empty. But I have learnt to despise my heart's yea and nay – God never changes.

Even if every work of grace in our heart seems conspicuous only by its absence, we may still say, 'I feel nothing whatever, but I believe God's deed of gift'. The infinite riches of this message are difficult to do justice to in words, the doors of the heart must be opened (Ephesians 1.18f). We have God as Father, Jesus as Brother, the Spirit as Paraclete, and a 'Kingdom of grace' – a Kingdom where we receive our citizenship free, by grace, and where we *live*, also by grace. We have deserved neither to enter or remain, but we are nevertheless allowed to stay.

It is, however, important to make clear that we are

speaking of solace for Christians in spiritual distress. The Good News can, unfortunately, be used as a soporific by those who refuse to pass through conviction, confession and conversion. The wonderful message of freedom in Christ must therefore be proclaimed in such a context that it will succour the distressed without becoming 'cheap grace' for those who say no to Jesus as Lord of their lives.

Scriptural testimonies

Those in spiritual darkness have always found solace in the fact that Scripture provides many examples of heroes of the faith who were themselves sorely tried. Abraham, David, Job, Jeremiah and the apostles all bear witness that the glory still lies ahead. We are not the first to suffer. Luther says that one of the marks of the believer in this world is 'the holy cross'; the Biblical figures who lived close to God all had their cross to bear.

> 'The heirs of salvation, I know from His word,
> Through much tribulation must follow their Lord.'

Baptism

As we have seen, we are charged with holding fast to the Word and the Gospel however unstable the feelings may be. The Lutheran tradition has always been concerned with teaching people to cling to the outward means of grace whereby Jesus comes to meet us – the sacraments. Among these baptism has a central place. Luther was eventually obliged by Zwingli and the enthusiasts to take the question up for thorough exposition. Baptism, he says, follows the baptised all his life; it is like a boat which we may, indeed, fall out of, but which nevertheless follows after us in the water. It is, therefore, our chance of rescue right up to death, for it contains God's promise of salvation addressed specially to each one of us, God's lifelong promise. This is why Luther is able to say that he comforts himself with his baptism – with the knowledge that the Gospel of Christ applies to him *personally*. God has granted me the Gospel already in my baptism – yes, to me!

> 'Baptism effects the forgiveness of sins, delivers from death and the devil and grants eternal salvation to all who believe, as the word and promise of God declare.'
> (Small Catechism)

The person who clings to Jesus in faith has all this as his own possession through baptism; Christ and His salvation come through the outward sign, we need not ascend into heaven to bring Him down. Baptism is therefore a source of comfort in the believer's spiritual distress.

Without a saving faith, however, baptism is harmful – says Luther. It is then a red light that warns us earnestly to stop, to repent. Pointing to the sacraments and at the same time living in sin and unbelief brings a man under yet greater condemnation. It is in spiritual trials that baptism is meant to comfort, for it belongs not to law but to Gospel, to grace.

Rosenius had to struggle with the question of baptism in order to deal with believer's-baptist tendencies among the Swedish revivalists, and wrote many letters of advice and counsel to people who had begun to have doubts on infant baptism. It was true, he said, that infant baptism could create a sense of false security in the unrepentant. But if we were to clear the world of all false comfort we would have to make away with God's grace, the perfect work of Christ, the Gospel and the Lord's Table – for all these were used much more often as tranquillisers than was baptism. Furthermore, abuse did not prevent there being a class of people who could properly seek solace in the fact of their baptism. We find vigorous Lutheran thinking in the following remarks:

'All that Christ *was*, *did* and *had* is given to us in baptism, transferred to us.'
'Baptism is at one and the same time a deed of union and a certificate of separation.'
'Christ has so totally united Himself with us and ourselves with Him that we may be and have what He is and has.'

In his hymns for 'anxious hearts', where he endeavours to lead condemned and hobbled consciences to freedom in Christ, Rosenius insists that baptism is the seal on Christ's purchase of our souls in His blood. This remains true, however sinful and feeble we know ourselves to be.

It is, of course, important to prevent people finding false assurance in baptism, and both Luther and Rosenius were concerned with this problem. If we do not have Christ as our goal we no longer have the Spirit and no longer enjoy baptismal grace; it is no use saying 'But I am baptised' *then* (c.f. 1 Corinthians 10.1–6).

The apostles, however, rarely mention baptism in direct connection with assurance, but frequently in the context of exhortations to a holy life, (see Romans 6.1f.). This should inspire caution and discrimination in our use of baptism as a solace.

The Lord's Table

Much the same applies to the Lord's Table. On the one hand we cannot emphasise too strongly that this is a sacrament, a means of grace, and as such may naturally be used to comfort the tried and distressed. Christ Himself is present in the Supper, and not only in a purely spiritual sense. All of Christ is given to us 'in, with and under' the bread and the wine. Whoever feels the sting of sin but feels, too, that Christ is hidden from him, may, in repentance and faith, grasp Him in the outward sign. Here He is, tactile – and for me!

Those who have their life in Christ and know the longing for Him that comes of being stripped of everything they had in themselves – they, too, can boldly comfort themselves with the gift of salvation they can receive in the outward sign.

'No guests at the Table are more fit and worthy to receive this heavenly food and drink given us at the Lord's Supper than those who come with a *wounded* and *broken* heart, a hungry and thirsty soul – even though they think themselves the most unworthy of all.' (Scriver)

On the other hand, a word of warning is equally necessary here. Without faith in the Saviour in our heart, we eat and drink our own damnation. A strongly 'realistic' sacramental theology – that is, the view that Jesus gives Himself to us in, with and under bread and wine – must not hinder us from turning the searchlight of self-examination on to our hearts and asking whether we will live with Him or no. The Lord's Supper is for God's people, not for the unconverted.

Confession

Confession – to another person – is less prominent among today's believers than it used to be, but we might usefully consider the discipline a fine solace for the sorely tried. The very act of opening the heart to a Christian brother or sister, whether priest, preacher or trusted layman, can in itself help to identify the problems and to correct perspectives.

The main purpose of the confessional is, however, the

personal granting of God's mercy for Jesus' sake. A fellow Christian tells us that God forgives us, yes, even us. If confession leads to a strengthened faith in the Word amid times of testing, it has been employed well and rightly. The decisive factor is confidence in God's word of grace – the word that the confessional takes and 'applies' personally.

The Christian Hope

The apostles were never afraid to comfort their converts with the hope of eternal life with God. 'Therefore encourage each other with these words' says Paul of his teachings on the Lord's return (1 Thess. 4.18). Elsewhere (Romans 5.5) he says that 'hope does not disappoint us'. As Christians we are pilgrims journeying onward, but we know that one day we will arrive; God will 'grant eternal life to me and to all who believe in Christ' (Small Catechism). Death is the final trial, and then there will be no more spiritual darknesses. The gospel of Christ is solace against death, for it gives us life everlasting. In distress and death we may direct our gaze forwards, in faith in Him who died for us. There, ahead, lies the kingdom of glory, where we shall experience the fulness of salvation and share in the glory of our God and Saviour Jesus Christ. God's purpose for our lives will then be attained.

Beyond death and the grave there are no trials, no distress, doubt or darkness. We must think ourselves forwards, the best lies onwards. Rosenius, too, wrote joyfully to his friends about that which awaited them on the other side of Jordan:

'Then shall I never more cry, fear and suffer from the power of sin within me, from the temptations and assaults of the devil, or from the world's malice, contempt, lies and disgrace. Think what this means –

I will suffer no more from sinful thoughts or desires,
but will be always holy, pure, free and spiritual –
waves of endless beatitude will bathe my heart.'

This longing in a Christian for blessedness is not a
selfish lust for pleasure, nor is it escapism, but it is a
work of the Holy Spirit. Solace in the Christian hope
should take its proper place in our hearts, for a living,
fighting faith cannot do without it.

Light in the darkness

Even though a true Christian will soon find that the trial
of faith is nothing abnormal in his life, he will also
discover that God comforts him with the Gospel and
sets his feet on firm ground. The Christian life is lived
in this tension between solace and tribulation, struggle
and victory, joy and sorrow, suffering and balm.

> 'Even though I walk through the valley of the
> shadow of death,
> I will fear no evil,
> for you are with me
> your rod and staff
> they comfort me.'   (Psalm 23.4)

The road to life is narrow and winds its way through
dark valleys. But in the midst of them it gives the
wayfarer that peace which is founded on assurance of
God's love and friendship – assurance of reconciliation
and unity with Him. This is the light in the darkness.

Conclusion

Not so long ago an old lay preacher remarked, 'I am
distressed when I hear of Christians who do not know
distress'. Let this be a warning first and foremost to our

teachers and preachers, for when they know how to confront people with the living God, experience of the trial of darkness will not be far behind. A sound exposition of Law and Gospel will make the doctrine of the sinful nature more than just theory – it will become a painful reality. And then the doctrine of Christ's sacrificial work will become more than just theory too, but something the poor sinner can cling to in life and death.

THE SPIRIT IS AMONG US: Personal Renewal and the Local Church

Philip Hacking

In this, his robust first book, Philip Hacking (Chairman of the Keswick Convention) contends for the local church as the true centre for revival and spiritual growth. As trendsetting as large celebration gatherings are, there is no substitute, he argues, for a committed Christian life lived in the context of a local fellowship of believers. Nor is there anything as thrilling as seeing the Spirit of God at work daily — developing spiritual depth and maturity in its members and establishing a bridgehead for God to reach the world with his truth. By returning to the New Testament pattern of worship, prayer, preaching and evangelism, Philip Hacking shows how every local church can become a focus for genuine personal renewal.

ON THE RIGHT TRACK: Contemporary Christians in Sport

John Searle, foreword by John Motson

'Killer instinct' is said to get sports stars to the top; but for Christians in sport it is their faith. Thirteen well-known figures from throughout the sporting world reveal here how they manage to combine burning ambition and Christian experience with integrity. Four-times Olympic winner Carl Lewis, ice-skating champion Nicky Slater, and world golf champion Gary Player are amongst them. And the story of the influential organisation Christians in Sport is also told.

If you wish to receive *regular*
information about *new books*,
please send your name and address
to:—
London Bible Warehouse
Po Box 123
Basingstoke
Hants RG23 7NL

Name:...

Address: ....

....

....

....

I am especially interested in:—

Music/Theology/"Popular"
Paperbacks
Delete which do not apply